LEADERSHIP IN TOUGH TIMES

SENIOR HOUSING: THE AI GAP

WORKBOOK

From Governance Theater to Deployment in 90 Days

Tools, Templates, and Vendor Intelligence
for Your Governance Committee

KEN LEATHERMAN
STORIFY STUDIOS | Newport, Oregon

Published by Storify Studios, Newport, Oregon.

www.storifystudios.com

> *Information current as of January 2026. Vendor details, pricing, and state regulations evolve rapidly — verify with vendors and legal counsel before acting.*

Companion to Senior Housing: The AI Gap

SECTION 1: HOW TO USE THIS WORKBOOK

Who this is for: Governance committees, implementation teams, executive sponsors, and anyone responsible for moving AI from discussion to deployment.

How it connects to the book: This workbook provides the operational tools referenced throughout Senior Housing: The AI Gap. The book provides the frameworks and strategy; this workbook provides the templates, checklists, calculators, and vendor intelligence to execute.

Workbook Section	Book Chapter	When to Use
Section 2: Vendor Landscape	Chapter 6	Week 3 of Sprint (vendor selection)
Section 3: Sprint Execution Kit	Chapter 14	Throughout the 90-Day AI Governance Sprint
Section 4: Contract Review	Chapters 7, 14	Week 4 of Sprint (before signing)
Section 5: Five Board Decisions	Chapter 11	Before starting Phase 4 pilots
Section 6: Maturity Model	Chapter 12	Before Sprint; reassess every 90 days
Section 7: ROI Calculators	Chapter 5	Pre-pilot business case + monthly tracking
Section 8: Data Quality & Integration	Chapters 7, 8	Week 1 of Sprint (infrastructure assessment)
Section 9: State Regulatory	Chapter 16	Pre-pilot compliance review
Section 10: Communication Templates	Chapter 13	Throughout implementation
Section 11: Compliance & Incident Response	Chapter 16	Pre-contract + ongoing monitoring
Section 12: Quick Reference Cards	All chapters	Ongoing reference

> *Note: Chapters 1–4 provide the strategic framework (the opportunity, the LITT Framework, failure modes, and governance theater). No operational tools are needed for those chapters — they inform your why before this workbook provides your how.*
>
> *Terminology note: This workbook uses "Stage 1, Stage 2, Stage 3" for the three stages within the 90-Day AI Governance Sprint. These are different from the four LITT Framework Phases (Phase 1–4). The entire Sprint occurs within LITT Phase 4 (Focus).*

How to Run a Committee Meeting Using This Workbook

1. Identify which Sprint week you're in
2. Open the corresponding Section 3 checklist
3. Review deliverables due this week
4. Use relevant templates from Sections 4–11 as needed
5. Document decisions and next steps

Update cycle: Review vendor profiles (Section 2) and state regulations (Section 9) annually. Templates and frameworks are evergreen.

SECTION 2: THE VENDOR LANDSCAPE BY CARE SETTING

2.1 Skilled Nursing Facilities

Clinical Documentation

Voize — Ambient AI clinical documentation

- Funding: $50M Series A (2025) | Launch: Early 2026 U.S. market
- Function: Voice-to-text documentation, auto-generates progress notes, care plan updates
- Cost: Estimated $100–$300 per provider per month
- Integration: Designed for major SNF EHR platforms
- Best For: Facilities with severe documentation burden (90+ min/shift charting)
- Contact: www.voize.com | Status: New market entrant, SNF-specific focus

Fall Detection & Prevention

SafelyYou — Computer vision AI fall detection

- Market Position: Market leader, extensive AL/SNF deployment
- Technology: Privacy-protected video analysis captures fall events only
- Cost: $250–$600 per bed annually
- Proven Results: Peer-reviewed research, industry-wide adoption
- Best For: Facilities with fall liability exposure, memory care units
- Contact: www.safely-you.com

CarePredict — Wearable fall detection + activity tracking

- Technology: Watch-style wearable with gesture recognition
- Advantage: No cameras (privacy benefit), tracks daily activity patterns
- Challenge: Resident compliance (must wear device)
- Cost: $200–$400 per bed annually
- Best For: Facilities where camera-based solutions face family resistance
- Contact: www.carepredict.com | Status: Vista Equity-backed

Inspiren (AUGi Device) — Geometric Exoskeletal Monitoring technology

- Funding: $35M Series A (March 2025)
- Technology: Wall-mounted devices + skeletal tracking
- Proven Metric: 90-second average response time
- Cost: $400–$700 per bed annually

- Best For: New construction or major renovations
- Contact: www.inspiren.com | Differentiator: Live visual context reduces false alarms

Platform Solutions

PointClickCare — Dominant SNF EHR (50%+ U.S. market share)

- AI Capabilities: Embedded analytics, predictive modeling, workflow automation, billing optimization
- Advantage: Already integrated — AI is an upgrade, not a new vendor
- Cost: Variable, typically $100–$200 per bed annually for AI features
- Contact: www.pointclickcare.com | Status: Public (NASDAQ: PCLK)

Aline (formerly Vitals) — Comprehensive platform via M&A

- Acquisitions: Vitals Software, Grove Menus, Roobrik
- AI Capabilities: Clinical documentation, nutrition management, admission screening
- Cost: Per-module, $50–$150 per bed per module annually
- Contact: www.aline.health | Status: PE-backed (Accel-KKR)

Analytics & Business Intelligence

SNF Metrics — Business intelligence and operational analytics

- AI Capabilities: Predictive staffing, fall prevention analytics, compliance monitoring, survey readiness
- Cost: $80–$150 per bed annually
- Contact: www.snfmetrics.com

Sparkco AI — Post-acute analytics, compliance automation

- Products: Real-time dashboards, automated compliance monitoring, survey readiness tools
- Cost: Enterprise pricing, varies by facility count
- Contact: www.sparkcoai.com

> *Predictive Analytics Note: Most predictive analytics are embedded in platform solutions (PointClickCare, Aline, SNF Metrics) rather than standalone. Cost: ~$50–$100 per bed annually as add-on. Use cases: 30-day readmission risk, sepsis detection, UTI prediction, health decline warnings. Requires clean data quality (see Section 8).*

SNF Prioritization Decision Tree

If your top pain point is...	Deploy first...	Expected ROI
Documentation burden (90+ min/shift)	Ambient documentation	3–6 months
2+ serious falls in past 12 months	Fall detection	Immediate
Labor costs >65% of revenue	Staffing optimization	6–9 months
Medicare denial rate >8%	Revenue cycle optimization	Immediate
None of the above	Fix operational fundamentals first	—

2.2 Assisted Living & Memory Care

EHR with AI Capabilities

ALIS (Assisted Living's Intelligent Software) — Ask ALIS: first AI-powered GPT for AL/MC/IL

- Launch: Q1 2026 general availability
- Function: Conversational AI for chart summaries, on-demand reports, voice-to-text charting
- Key Features: 20+ language support, context-aware, native to platform
- Security: HITRUST compliant
- Cost: $15–$30 per resident monthly
- Contact: www.alis.io | Status: Purpose-built for AL

ResiDex — All-in-one EHR for AL/MC/IL

- Ownership: Accel-KKR (PE)
- Functions: Care plans, eMAR, incident tracking, billing, CRM
- Cost: $12–$25 per resident monthly
- Contact: www.residex.com | Status: Mature product, large customer base

Resident Engagement & Life Enrichment

TSOLife — AI-populated resident profiles

- Funding: $43M Series B (May 2025, PeakSpan)
- Function: Mobile app records resident interviews, AI populates comprehensive profiles
- Value: Transforms 3–4 hour intake into 30–45 minute process
- Cost: $5–$12 per resident monthly
- Contact: www.tsolife.com

LifeLoop — Resident engagement hub

- Ownership: Vista Equity Partners (2023)
- Functions: Activity calendars, family chat, fall-alert dashboards, task management
- Acquisition: Linked Senior (July 2024) adds evidence-based programming
- Cost: $8–$15 per resident monthly
- Contact: www.lifeloop.com

Safety Systems

Fall Detection: SafelyYou, Inspiren, CarePredict (see SNF section)

RF Technologies — Wander management

- Ownership: SRM Equity (PE)

- Products: Wander-management badges, wall-mounted fall detection, emergency call
- Cost: $300–$600 per bed annually for comprehensive suite
- Best For: Memory care units requiring integrated safety
- Contact: www.rfsmart.com

Skypoint (Senior Living 365) — Unified platform (50+ applications)

- Features: 350+ KPIs, AI-powered forecasting, 360-degree resident view
- Security: HITRUST r2 certified
- Cost: Enterprise, $75–$150 per bed annually
- Contact: www.skypointcloud.com

AL/MC Prioritization Decision Tree

If your top pain point is...	Deploy first...	Expected ROI
Paper medication systems	eMAR platform	6–12 months
Memory care without wander mgmt.	Wander management	Immediate
Engagement scores below market	Engagement platform	6–12 months
Underbilling for care delivered	Care level assessment	3–6 months

2.3 Independent Living

IL predominantly uses consumer-grade technology rather than specialized vendors.

Voice Assistants: Amazon Alexa ($50–$200), Google Home ($50–$200), Apple HomePod ($300+). Offer optional setup, don't mandate platform.

Smart Home: Smart thermostats ($150–$300), smart lighting ($20–$100/room), door/window sensors ($30–$80). Prioritize Matter-compatible devices.

Fall Detection (Consumer): Apple Watch Series 4+ ($400–$800), medical alert systems ($30–$50/mo.), ambient sensors: Nobi ($2,000+), Walabot Home ($200–$300).

Companion AI: ElliQ ($250 + $30/mo.), Eve (phone-based). Pilot with 10–15 interested residents, opt-in only.

IL Prioritization Decision Tree

If your top priority is...	Deploy first...	Expected Investment
WiFi is slow/unreliable	Infrastructure upgrade	$50K–$150K
Falls causing IL-to-AL transfers	Fall detection education + group purchasing	Varies
Residents requesting smart home	Tiered smart apartment packages	Start with models
Social isolation concerns	Companion AI pilot	$250 + $30/mo/unit

2.4 Home Care

Sensi.ai — 24/7 AI care copilot

- Function: Monitors physical/emotional/cognitive needs through home sensors
- Cost: $30–$75 per client monthly
- Best For: High-acuity clients with hospitalization risk
- Contact: www.sensi.ai

CareAlert — AI sensors for activity/safety monitoring (no cameras)

- Technology: Motion sensors, pattern detection
- Cost: $159 one-time, no monthly fee
- Contact: www.carealert.com

Mobile Documentation Platforms: AlayaCare, ClearCare (WellSky), Homecare Homebase, Smartcare. Common features: voice-to-text, GPS verification, family portals, offline capability. Cost: $30–$60/caregiver/month.

Home Care Prioritization

Priority	Deploy...	Timeline
1	Mobile documentation + GPS verification	Within 90 days
2	Scheduling optimization	After documentation digital
3	AI-driven training platforms	After scheduling optimized
4	Client monitoring (opt-in, premium)	When capacity allows

2.5 Vendor Evaluation Matrix

Rate each criterion 1–5. Calculate the weighted total.

Category (Weight)	Criterion	Weight	Vendor A	Vendor B	Vendor C
Product (30%)	Core Functionality	10%	__/5	__/5	__/5
	AI Performance	10%	__/5	__/5	__/5
	Scalability	10%	__/5	__/5	__/5
Integration (25%)	EHR Integration	10%	__/5	__/5	__/5
	Technical Architecture	8%	__/5	__/5	__/5
	Data Security	7%	__/5	__/5	__/5
Implementation (20%)	Timeline	7%	__/5	__/5	__/5
	Training & Change Mgmt.	7%	__/5	__/5	__/5
	Technical Support	6%	__/5	__/5	__/5
Viability (15%)	Financial Stability	8%	__/5	__/5	__/5
	Market Position	7%	__/5	__/5	__/5
Cost (10%)	Pricing Transparency	5%	__/5	__/5	__/5
	ROI Potential	5%	__/5	__/5	__/5
	WEIGHTED TOTAL		_____	_____	_____

> *Scoring: 4.0–5.0 = Excellent | 3.0–3.9 = Acceptable | 2.0–2.9 = Concerns | <2.0 = Do not proceed*

2.6 Vendor Due Diligence Checklist

Documentation Required

- ☐ Customer references (3–5 similar facilities)
- ☐ Implementation timeline
- ☐ Training materials
- ☐ Business Associate Agreement (BAA)
- ☐ SOC 2 / HITRUST certification
- ☐ FDA clearance (if applicable)
- ☐ Integration documentation for YOUR EHR
- ☐ All-in pricing breakdown
- ☐ Sample contract
- ☐ Security policies
- ☐ Breach response plan
- ☐ Product roadmap

Verification Steps

- ☐ Called 2–3 references
- ☐ Verified performance claims
- ☐ Confirmed integration works with your EHR
- ☐ BAA reviewed by legal counsel
- ☐ HIPAA compliance documented
- ☐ State AI compliance verified
- ☐ Pilot exit clause included
- ☐ Integration guaranteed in writing
- ☐ Data ownership confirmed
- ☐ Budget approved
- ☐ Executive sponsor confirmed
- ☐ IT consulted
- ☐ Legal reviewed
- ☐ Risk management comfortable

> *Sign only after ALL items checked.*

2.7 EHR Compatibility Quick Reference

Use this table to identify which AI vendors have confirmed integration with your EHR platform.

AI Tool	PointClickCare	ALIS	ResiDex	MatrixCare	Netsmart	AlayaCare
Voize	✓	—	—	TBD	TBD	—
SafelyYou	✓	✓	—	✓	—	—
CarePredict	✓	—	—	✓	—	—
Inspiren	✓	—	—	✓	—	—
SNF Metrics	✓	—	—	✓	—	—
TSOLife	—	✓	✓	—	—	—
LifeLoop	—	✓	✓	—	—	—
Sensi.ai	—	—	—	—	—	✓

> *✓ = Confirmed integration | — = Not available / not confirmed | TBD = In development*

>

> *IMPORTANT: "Integration" claims vary from full bidirectional data flow to one-way data export. Always verify with the Five Questions That Matter (Section 8.1). This table reflects publicly available information as of January 2026 and should be verified directly with vendors.*

SECTION 3: THE 90-DAY AI GOVERNANCE SPRINT EXECUTION KIT

3.1 Pre-Sprint Readiness Assessment

Facility Name: ____________________

Assessment Date: ____________________

Operational Reality

1. Biggest operational pain point: ____________________

Estimated annual cost: $ ____________________

2. How long have you discussed without taking action? ____________________

3. What have we tried? What happened? ____________________

Organizational Readiness

4. Staff champions willing to pilot?

☐ Yes ☐ No

Names: ____________________

5. Executive Sponsor: ____________________

☐ Will attend weekly check-ins

☐ Will delegate (RED FLAG)

6. Can staff give honest feedback without fear?

☐ Yes ☐ No

Data & Infrastructure

7. Is the data quality adequate for AI? (Complete Section 8, Data Quality Assessment, for details)

☐ Yes ☐ No ☐ Unknown

8. WIFI/network adequate?

☐ Yes ☐ No

Budget

9. Approved pilot budget: $ ____________________

☐ Accessible within 30 days

10. Budget authority: ____________________

Additional approvals needed: ____________________

Red Flags (check any that apply)

- ☐ No executive sponsor for weekly check-ins
- ☐ Staff openly hostile to technology
- ☐ No budget approved or accessible
- ☐ Data too poor for any AI tool
- ☐ Procurement requires 6+ months

Red flag count: ____________________

> *If 2+ red flags, address before starting Sprint.*

READINESS: ☐ Ready ☐ Nearly Ready (1–2 gaps) ☐ Not Ready

Approved by Committee: ____________________

3.2 Stage 1: Days 1–30

Week 1: Brutal Truth Assessment

- ☐ Convene governance committee (or form one)
- ☐ Schedule weekly meetings for the Sprint duration
- ☐ Assign an executive sponsor who will attend every meeting
- ☐ Complete Readiness Assessment (3.1 above)
- ☐ Complete Data Quality Assessment (Section 8.2)
- ☐ Identify the biggest pain points costing money/quality
- ☐ Document staff readiness using 10-80-10 framework (Section 12.3)
- ☐ Confirm budget availability ($25K–$75K typical)

Deliverable: ☐ One-page Current State Assessment approved

Week 2: Pain Point Selection

Pain Point Scoring Matrix

Use Case	Impact (1–5)	Scope (1–5)	Measurable (1–5)	Total
____________	___	___	___	___
____________	___	___	___	___
____________	___	___	___	___
____________	___	___	___	___

- ☐ Interviewed 3–5 frontline staff
- ☐ Selected ONE use case: ____________

- ☐ Problem statement documented
- ☐ Current state metrics defined
- ☐ Success criteria defined

Deliverable: ☐ Pilot Use Case Definition (1–2 pages) approved

Week 3: Vendor Short List

- ☐ Researched 5–7 vendors (use Section 2)
- ☐ Verified senior housing experience
- ☐ Checked security compliance
- ☐ Requested demos from the top 3
- ☐ Invited frontline staff to demos
- ☐ Standardized demo questions

Vendor Comparison Matrix

Use Case: ____________________

Criterion	Vendor A	Vendor B	Vendor C
Addresses use case?	☐Y☐N	☐Y☐N	☐Y☐N
Sr housing facilities served	____	____	____
References provided	____	____	____
Works with our EHR?	☐Y☐N	☐Y☐N	☐Y☐N
Bidirectional data?	☐Y☐N	☐Y☐N	☐Y☐N
Integration timeline	____ days	____ days	____ days
BAA provided?	☐Y☐N	☐Y☐N	☐Y☐N
HITRUST/SOC 2?	☐Y☐N	☐Y☐N	☐Y☐N
Pilot cost	$____	$____	$____
Enterprise cost	$____	$____	$____
Training included?	☐Y☐N	☐Y☐N	☐Y☐N
Years in business	____	____	____
Overall Score	___/5	___/5	___/5

Deliverable: ☐ Vendor Comparison Matrix with recommendation

Week 4: Pilot Design

- ☐ Selected vendor
- ☐ Called customer references
- ☐ Completed Integration Evaluation (Section 8.1)
- ☐ Completed HIPAA Vendor Compliance Verification (Section 11.1)
- ☐ Defined pilot scope
- ☐ Established baseline metrics
- ☐ Designed training using role-specific approach (Section 10.7)
- ☐ Created budget breakdown
- ☐ Secured budget approval
- ☐ Drafted communication plan (Section 10)
- ☐ Developed risk mitigation
- ☐ Reviewed contract using checklists (Section 4)
- ☐ Scheduled pilot start for Week 5

PILOT DESIGN DOCUMENT

Project: ______________________________

PM: ______________________________

Scope

Parameter	Detail
Unit/Location	__________________
Beds	____
Staff roles/count	__________________
Training hours/person	____
Start date	__________________
Duration	____ days

Success Metrics

Metric	Baseline	Target	Method
Primary 1: ____	____	____	____
Primary 2: ____	____	____	____
Staff satisfaction	N/A	≥3.5/5	Survey
Uptime	N/A	>95%	Vendor

Budget

Item	Cost
Vendor pilot fee	$____
Implementation	$____
Staff training (internal)	$____
IT integration	$____
Project management	$____
Contingency (10–20%)	$____
TOTAL	$____

Decision Criteria (Week 12):

- ☐ Primary metrics ____% improvement
- ☐ Staff adoption >____%
- ☐ ROI payback <____ months
- ☐ Technology performs as promised
- ☐ No major safety/compliance issues

Signatures: Sponsor ______________________________

3.3 Stage 2: Days 31–60

Week 5: Pilot Launch

- ☐ Vendor deploys technology
- ☐ Staff training completed (hands-on, role-specific)
- ☐ Staff communication sent (Section 10.1)
- ☐ Family FAQ distributed (Section 10.3)
- ☐ Resident information sheet posted (Section 10.4)
- ☐ Baseline metrics documented
- ☐ Executive sponsor visits pilot unit Day 31–32
- ☐ Daily check-ins with staff (15 min)
- ☐ Support contact established
- ☐ Metrics tracking initiated
- ☐ Day 1 issues documented

Deliverable: ☐ Pilot LIVE and operational

Weeks 6–7: Execution & Support

- ☐ Daily check-ins Week 6 → weekly Week 7
- ☐ Issues resolved within 24 hours
- ☐ Staff feedback collected
- ☐ Usage/adoption tracked
- ☐ Metrics tracked vs. baseline
- ☐ Small wins celebrated publicly

Weekly Status Report (use Weeks 6–11)

Week: ____________________

Metric	Baseline	Current	Change	Trend
Primary 1	___	___	___%	↑↓→
Primary 2	___	___	___%	↑↓→
Staff Usage	N/A	___%	N/A	↑↓→

Working well: ____________________

Needs improvement: ____________________

Overall: ☐ On Track ☐ At Risk ☐ Off Track

Week 8: Mid-Pilot Assessment

- ☐ Reviewed all metrics
- ☐ Staff satisfaction survey conducted
- ☐ Technology performing as promised?
- ☐ Resident/family feedback gathered
- ☐ Vendor responsive to issues?

Decision: ☐ Continue ☐ Adjust ☐ Abort

If adjusting: ____________________

If aborting: ____________________

Deliverable: ☐ Mid-Point Assessment Memo

3.4 Stage 3: Days 61–90

Weeks 9–10: Data Collection & Analysis

- ☐ Final metrics vs. baseline
- ☐ ROI calculated (Section 7)
- ☐ Usage data compiled
- ☐ 5–10 staff interviews conducted (use Staff Interview Guide below)
- ☐ Resident/family feedback gathered
- ☐ Vendor performance evaluated
- ☐ Lessons learned documented

Staff Interview Guide

Staff: ____________________

1. Frequency of use: ☐ Daily ☐ Several/week ☐ Weekly ☐ Rarely ☐ Never
2. Ease of use (1–5): ______
3. Job impact: ☐ Much easier ☐ Somewhat easier ☐ No change ☐ Harder ☐ Much harder
4. What worked well? ____________________
5. What frustrated you? ____________________
6. Continue facility-wide? ☐ Yes ☐ Probably ☐ Unsure ☐ Probably not ☐ No
7. What would you change? ____________________
8. Recommend to peers? __________
9. Training quality (1–5): ______
10. Support quality (1–5): ______

Deliverable: ☐ Pilot Results Report (8–12 pages)

Week 11: Stakeholder Review

- ☐ Presented to governance committee
- ☐ Presented to frontline staff
- ☐ Presented to executive leadership
- ☐ Board briefed if appropriate
- ☐ Consensus built
- ☐ Recommendation refined

Week 12: Scale Decision

☐ Scale Decision Meeting held (90 min max)

Decision made: ☐ SCALE ☐ PIVOT ☐ STOP

Rationale: ____________________

If scaling: Units ____________________

If pivoting: Plan ____________________

If stopping: Lessons ____________________

Next steps owner: ____________________

☐ Decision communicated to all stakeholders within 48 hours

> *"Let's discuss more at the next meeting" is NOT acceptable.*

3.5 Scale Decision Framework

See Senior Housing: The AI Gap Chapter 15 for the strategic framework behind these patterns.

Recognizing Your Pattern

Review your pilot data against these twelve patterns to identify your situation and the correct decision.

SCALE Patterns (20%+ improvement on primary metrics):

Pattern	What You See	Decision
1. Clear Success	All metrics exceed targets, staff enthusiastic, technology stable	Scale immediately
2. Strong Success, Fixable Issues	Primary metrics strong, minor workflow problems identified	Scale with fixes — document issues, set correction timeline
3. Partial Success, Expandable	Works well for specific use case, other applications untested	Scale the proven use case, pilot additional applications separately

PIVOT Patterns (10–20% improvement, or mixed results):

Pattern	What You See	Decision
4. Right Problem, Wrong Vendor	Clear need confirmed, vendor underperforms	Switch vendors, retain use case, accelerate evaluation
5. Right Vendor, Wrong Use Case	Technology works, but chosen problem wasn't the real pain point	Redeploy same vendor on higher-value use case
6. Right Everything, Wrong Unit	Technology and use case work, but pilot unit had unique barriers	Repeat pilot on better-suited unit
7. Timing Issue	Organization wasn't ready (data quality, change management gaps)	Fix readiness gaps, restart Sprint in 90 days

STOP Patterns (<10% improvement, or negative results):

Pattern	What You See	Decision
8. Technology Failure	System doesn't perform as promised, vendor can't fix	Stop. Document vendor shortcomings. Evaluate alternatives.
9. Cultural Rejection	Staff refuse adoption despite training and support	Stop AI pilot. Address culture first (Chapter 9). Restart later.
10. No Real Problem	Pilot reveals the problem wasn't significant enough to justify AI	Stop. Redirect resources to real pain points.
11. Compliance Risk	Regulatory concerns emerge that can't be resolved	Stop immediately. Consult legal.
12. Financial Non-Viability	Costs exceed benefits with no path to positive ROI	Stop. Consider lower-cost alternatives.

Scale Decision Quantitative Thresholds

Metric	Scale	Pivot	Stop
Primary metric improvement	20%+	10–20%	<10%
Staff adoption rate	>70% daily use	40–70%	<40%
Staff satisfaction	≥3.5/5	2.5–3.4/5	<2.5/5
Technology uptime	>95%	90–95%	<90%
ROI trajectory	Positive within 12 mo	Breakeven 12–24 mo	No path to positive

Scale Business Case Template (7–9 Pages Maximum)

> *Boards won't read 50-page proposals. Keep it tight.*

Page 1: Executive Summary (1 page)

- Pilot results in three sentences
- Recommendation (scale/pivot/stop)
- Investment required and expected return
- Timeline

Page 2: Pilot Results (1 page)

- Metrics: baseline vs. results vs. targets (table format)
- Staff adoption and satisfaction data
- Technology performance
- Unexpected findings

Page 3: Financial Analysis (1 page)

- Pilot costs vs. budget
- Measured benefits (documented, not projected)
- Enterprise deployment cost projection
- 24-month ROI projection with sensitivity analysis

Page 4: Scale Plan (1 page)

- Phase 1: Department expansion (months 4–6) — units, timeline, budget
- Phase 2: Facility-wide (months 7–12) — scope, resources, milestones
- Phase 3: Portfolio (months 13–18, if applicable) — standardization plan

Page 5: Risk Assessment (1 page)

- Top 5 risks with likelihood, impact, and mitigation
- Compliance status
- Vendor viability assessment

Page 6: Resource Requirements (1 page)

- Budget by phase (table)
- Staff time requirements
- IT/infrastructure needs
- Training plan

Page 7: Implementation Roadmap (1 page)

Phase	Timeline	Key Milestones	Budget	Go/No-Go Criteria
Department Expansion	Months 4–6	___	$___	___
Facility-Wide	Months 7–12	___	$___	___
Portfolio	Months 13–18	___	$___	___
Optimization	Months 19+	___	$___	___

Pages 8–9: Appendices (optional)

- Staff survey results summary
- Vendor performance data
- Comparable facility results (if available)

Scale Decision Meeting Agenda

Duration: 90 minutes maximum

Time	Agenda Item	Lead
0:00–0:10	Opening: Sprint objectives and process review	Committee Chair
0:10–0:20	Pilot Results Presentation	Project Manager
0:20–0:30	Financial Analysis	Finance Lead
0:30–0:40	Staff and Stakeholder Feedback	HR/Operations Lead
0:40–0:50	Recommendation and Scale Plan	Project Manager
0:50–1:10	Discussion	All
1:10–1:20	Decision Vote	Committee Chair
1:20–1:30	Communication Planning (who tells whom, by when)	Committee Chair

Facilitation Guide:

- Distribute the business case 48 hours before the meeting — no cold reads
- Begin with data, not opinions
- Address the elephant: "Based on the evidence, should we scale, pivot, or stop?"
- Require every committee member to state a position before discussion
- If no consensus after 20 minutes of discussion, the executive sponsor decides
- Document the decision, rationale, and next steps before anyone leaves the room
- Communicate the decision to all stakeholders within 48 hours

> *A decision to stop is a success. It means the Sprint worked — you tested, learned, and made an evidence-based decision instead of drifting into permanent piloting.*

3.6 Scale Readiness Checklist

Complete before enterprise expansion.

Technology

- ☐ Vendor supports volume (in writing)
- ☐ Integration tested at scale
- ☐ Security verified for expanded scope
- ☐ Disaster recovery plans documented
- ☐ Monitoring tools deployed

Operational

- ☐ Training program scalable and repeatable
- ☐ Support model defined for expanded deployment

- ☐ Change management plan per unit
- ☐ Communication templates ready (Section 10)
- ☐ Process documentation updated

Financial

- ☐ Budget approved for expansion
- ☐ Hidden costs identified and budgeted
- ☐ ROI model validated against pilot data
- ☐ Scale pricing negotiated with vendor
- ☐ Payment aligned with rollout milestones

Governance

- ☐ Executive sponsor confirmed for expansion
- ☐ Steering committee committed to continued oversight
- ☐ KPIs defined for scale deployment
- ☐ Accountability assigned by unit
- ☐ Risk plan documented and updated

Staff

- ☐ Champions identified per unit
- ☐ Training time scheduled
- ☐ Resistance plan developed
- ☐ Recognition program established
- ☐ Feedback mechanisms in place

Data

- ☐ Quality standards enforced across expansion scope
- ☐ Governance policies documented
- ☐ Integration tested for new units
- ☐ Reporting ready for expanded metrics
- ☐ Security extended to new users/locations

Stakeholder

- ☐ Board supportive of expansion investment
- ☐ Resident/family communication plan finalized

- ☐ Regulatory compliance confirmed for expanded scope
- ☐ Insurance updated (cyber liability, professional liability)
- ☐ External partners aligned

Vendor

- ☐ Implementation plan agreed for expansion phases
- ☐ Vendor resources committed
- ☐ Escalation path defined
- ☐ Performance guarantees in place
- ☐ Post-implementation support confirmed

Total: ____________________

> *35–40: Ready to scale | 28–34: Address gaps first | <28: Not ready — resolve deficiencies*

SECTION 4: CONTRACT REVIEW & VENDOR MANAGEMENT

4.1 Pre-Signature Process

1. Obtain complete contract package (master agreement, BAA, SLAs, pricing, exhibits)
2. Review using checklists below — document concerns
3. Share with legal counsel
4. Negotiate changes
5. Obtain final executed contract
6. Store securely

> *Allow 2–4 weeks for review and negotiation before pilot start.*

4.2 BAA Checklist

NON-NEGOTIABLE if AI touches PHI. See Senior Housing: The AI Gap Chapter 16: No BAA = No Contract.

- ☐ BAA provided without resistance (RED FLAG if vendor hesitates)
- ☐ Permitted uses defined — services only, no marketing/research/sale
- ☐ Safeguards specified — administrative, physical, technical
- ☐ Sub-contractor flow-down — cloud providers covered, you know who they are
- ☐ Breach notification — 24–72 hours, details provided, vendor assists
- ☐ Audit rights — request documentation, SOC 2/HITRUST reports
- ☐ Data return/destruction — 30–60 days, secure deletion, certified in writing
- ☐ Liability allocation — vendor indemnifies for vendor-caused breaches
- ☐ BAA consistent with master agreement — BAA controls for HIPAA matters
- ☐ AI training data provisions — vendor must disclose if/how your data trains AI models
- ☐ Sub-processor disclosure — list of all cloud providers handling PHI (AWS, Azure, Google Cloud)
- ☐ BAA chain verified — vendor has BAAs with all sub-processors

> *DEAL-BREAKER: No adequate BAA = no contract if PHI is involved.*

4.3 Core Contract Checklist

Scope

- ☐ Services clearly defined (license vs. SaaS, implementation, training, support, updates)
- ☐ Deliverables with acceptance criteria
- ☐ Exclusions stated
- ☐ Change order process

Implementation

- ☐ Timeline with milestone dates and delay consequences
- ☐ Vendor responsibilities (PM, configuration, integration, training, testing)
- ☐ Your responsibilities (access, IT, staff, decisions)
- ☐ Integration specifications (systems, method, data fields, testing)
- ☐ Acceptance testing (plan, criteria, period, right to reject)
- ☐ Pilot exit clause — terminate within pilot, refund provisions, data return, no penalty

SLAs

- ☐ Uptime: 99.9% strong | 99.5% acceptable | 99.0% weak
- ☐ Response times: Critical 1–2hr 24/7 | High 4–8hr | Medium 1–2 days | Low 3–5 days
- ☐ "Response" vs. "resolution" clarified
- ☐ SLA failure consequences (credits, termination rights)

Pricing

- ☐ All costs itemized (no surprises)
- ☐ Payment tied to deliverables
- ☐ Annual increase capped (3–5%, CPI)
- ☐ Enterprise pricing locked if pilot converts
- ☐ Refund provisions

Data

- ☐ You own your data
- ☐ No secondary use without permission
- ☐ U.S. data centers
- ☐ Standard export formats
- ☐ Return upon termination (30–60 days, machine-readable, no fees)

- ☐ Deletion after return (certified)
- ☐ No use of your data to train AI models without explicit written consent

Security

- ☐ SOC 2 Type II minimum, HITRUST preferred
- ☐ Encryption: TLS 1.2+ transit, AES-256 rest
- ☐ Role-based access, MFA
- ☐ Annual penetration testing
- ☐ Breach response plan
- ☐ Cyber liability insurance ($1M min, $5M+ preferred)
- ☐ Your audit rights

Term & Termination

- ☐ Initial term defined
- ☐ Auto-renewal notice period calendared
- ☐ Termination for convenience (minimize early termination fees)
- ☐ Termination for cause (breach defined, 30-day cure, no penalty)
- ☐ Transition assistance (60–90 day access, data return)

Liability

- ☐ Caps reasonable (exceptions for BAA breach, IP, gross negligence)
- ☐ Vendor indemnifies for IP infringement, HIPAA violations, negligence
- ☐ Performance representations in contract (not just marketing)

4.4 AI-Specific Contract Provisions

These provisions are unique to AI contracts and frequently missing from standard vendor agreements.

- ☐ Algorithm transparency: Vendor discloses how AI makes decisions (or explains why proprietary)
- ☐ Bias testing: Vendor provides evidence of bias testing for your population (age, cognitive status, race)
- ☐ Model updates: How and when AI models are updated; advance notice requirements; your right to test before deployment
- ☐ Performance degradation: What happens if AI performance declines over time; vendor obligation to maintain accuracy

☐ FDA status: If clinical AI, vendor provides FDA clearance documentation or explains why not required

☐ Human override: Contract confirms human override capability is maintained at all times

☐ Audit trail: AI decisions are logged with reasoning for regulatory compliance

☐ Training data provenance: Vendor discloses training data sources and confirms proper consent/de-identification

4.5 Post-Signature Management

☐ Contract stored securely

☐ Renewal deadlines calendared (set reminder 90 days before)

☐ Key stakeholders have copies

☐ Performance monitored monthly against SLAs

☐ Issues documented with dates and resolution

☐ Annual review scheduled

Quarterly Vendor Review (30 min):

1. SLA performance review
2. Open issues status
3. Usage metrics
4. Product updates and roadmap
5. Integration health check
6. Action items with owners and deadlines

SECTION 5: THE FIVE BOARD DECISIONS TOOLKIT

> *Complete before starting Phase 4 pilots. See Senior Housing: The AI Gap Chapter 11: The Five Board Decisions for Senior Housing.*

5.1 Decision 1: AI Boundaries

For each area, check the maximum authorized AI level:

Application	L1: Data Aggregator	L2: Decision Support	L3: Conditional Auto	L4: Autonomous
Clinical documentation	☐	☐	☐	☐
Fall detection/monitoring	☐	☐	☐	☐
Care planning	☐	☐	☐	☐
Medication management	☐	☐	☐	☐
Staffing/scheduling	☐	☐	☐	☐
Billing/revenue cycle	☐	☐	☐	☐
Resident engagement	☐	☐	☐	☐
Admissions screening	☐	☐	☐	☐

> *L1: AI collects/presents data, humans decide. L2: AI recommends, humans review. L3: AI acts within parameters, humans oversee. L4: AI acts independently (not recommended for clinical).*

Boundary Classification by Care Setting

Application	SNF Recommended Max	AL/MC Recommended Max	IL Recommended Max	Home Care Recommended Max
Clinical documentation	L3	L3	N/A	L2
Fall detection	L3	L3	L1 (opt-in)	L2
Care planning	L2	L2	N/A	L2
Medication management	L2	L2	N/A	L1
Staffing/scheduling	L3	L3	L1	L3
Billing/revenue cycle	L3	L2	L1	L2
Resident engagement	L2	L2	L2	L1
Behavioral monitoring	L2	L3 (MC) / L2 (AL)	Not recommended	L1

> *These are starting recommendations. Your board may adjust based on organizational capacity, risk tolerance, and regulatory environment. Memory care may warrant higher monitoring levels due to safety imperatives; IL requires lower levels due to resident autonomy expectations.*

Board Resolution: "The Board authorizes AI at Level

....

Approved: ....

5.2 Decision 2: Risk Tolerance

Application	Max False Negative	Max False Positive	Rationale
Fall detection	____% (missed falls)	____% (false alarms)	____
Deterioration alerts	____% (missed events)	____% (unnecessary alerts)	____
Documentation accuracy	____% (errors)	N/A	____
Staffing predictions	____% (understaffed)	____% (overstaffed)	____
Billing/coding	____% (undercoded)	____% (overcoded)	____

Risk Tolerance Guidance

Application	Conservative	Moderate	Aggressive
Fall detection (false negative)	<2%	<5%	<8%
Fall detection (false positive)	<15%	<25%	<35%
Clinical alerts (false negative)	<3%	<5%	<10%
Documentation accuracy	>98%	>95%	>90%
Staffing (understaffed shifts)	<5%	<10%	<15%
Billing (overcoding rate)	<1%	<2%	<3%

> *Clinical applications require conservative thresholds. Administrative applications can tolerate moderate risk. Start conservative and adjust based on evidence.*

Approved: ....

5.3 Decision 3: Human Accountability

Level	Role	Responsible For	Escalation Trigger
Point-of-Care	____	Validating AI, overriding when needed	AI contradicts clinical judgment
Administrative	____	Monitoring performance, reporting	Pattern of errors
Executive	____	Resources, vendor mgmt, strategy	System-level failures
Board	____	Policy, risk tolerance, investment	Regulatory/safety events

RACI Chart for AI Systems

Activity	Point-of-Care	Admin	Executive	Board	IT	Vendor
Daily AI validation	R	I	—	—	—	—
Override decisions	R/A	I	I (if pattern)	—	—	—
Performance monitoring	C	R	A	I	C	C
Incident investigation	C	R	A	I (if serious)	C	R
System maintenance	—	—	—	—	R	R/A
Policy updates	—	C	R	A	C	I
Budget decisions	—	C	R	A	C	—
Vendor management	—	C	R/A	I	C	—

> *R = Responsible (does the work) | A = Accountable (final authority) | C = Consulted | I = Informed*

Incident Response Escalation:

Override → notify admin (1 hr.) → root cause (24 hr.) → executive brief (72 hr.) → corrective action (1 wk.) → board if safety/regulatory event

Approved: ______________________________

5.4 Decision 4: Data Governance

Policy Area	Decision	Details
Collection	What can AI collect?	☐ Clinical ☐ Behavioral ☐ Location ☐ Financial
Retention	How long kept?	____ months/years
Resident Access	Can residents see AI data?	☐ On request ☐ Portal ☐ No
Family Access	Can families see AI data?	☐ With consent ☐ POA/guardian ☐ No
Vendor Access	What can vendors do?	☐ Services only ☐ Anonymized ☐ No secondary
Sharing	External sharing?	☐ Regulators only ☐ De-identified ☐ Never
Deletion	When/how deleted?	Trigger: ____ Method: ____
Opt-Out	Can residents opt out?	☐ All AI ☐ Specific systems ☐ No

Data Governance Policy Template

Section 1: Purpose. This policy establishes governance for all AI systems processing resident, staff, or operational data at [Facility Name].

Section 2: Scope. Applies to all AI tools, machine learning systems, and automated decision-support technologies used in any capacity.

Section 3: Data Classification.

Classification	Examples	Handling Requirements
PHI	Health records, diagnoses, medications	HIPAA-compliant, BAA required, encrypted
PII	Names, SSN, financial data	Encrypted, access-controlled, minimized
Operational	Staffing patterns, census data, costs	Access-controlled, internal use only
De-identified	Aggregated trends, anonymized analytics	May be shared per data use agreement

Section 4: Collection Principles. Collect only what is necessary for the specific AI use case. Document what is collected and why. Inform residents and families.

Section 5: Access Controls. Role-based access. Multi-factor authentication. Audit logging. Automatic session timeouts. Quarterly access reviews.

Section 6: Vendor Requirements. All vendors handling data must sign BAAs (if PHI), provide SOC 2 or HITRUST certification, agree to data return/destruction on termination, and disclose sub-processors.

Section 7: Incident Response. See Section 11 of this workbook for complete incident response protocols.

Section 8: Review. This policy reviewed annually by governance committee. Updated when new AI systems are deployed or regulations change.

Approved: ______________________________

5.5 Decision 5: Investment Commitment

Phase	Timeline	Budget	Go/No-Go Criteria	Authority
Pilot	Day 1–90	$___	Success criteria met	Committee
Department	Month 4–9	$___	ROI confirmed, adoption >___%	Executive
Enterprise	Month 10–18	$___	Dept ROI validated, stable	Board
Portfolio	Month 19+	$___	Enterprise proven	Board

Budget Tracker

Line	Approved	Spent	Remaining	Variance
Vendor fees	$___	$___	$___	___%
Implementation	$___	$___	$___	___%
Training	$___	$___	$___	___%
IT/Integration	$___	$___	$___	___%
PM	$___	$___	$___	___%
Contingency	$___	$___	$___	___%
TOTAL	$___	$___	$___	___%

Investment Go/No-Go Decision Matrix

Signal	Proceed	Pause	Stop
ROI trajectory	Positive or on track	Flat, needs more data	Negative, no path to positive
Staff adoption	>70% and growing	40–70%, stable	<40% or declining
Technology stability	<5% downtime	5–10% downtime	>10% or critical failures
Regulatory status	Compliant, no concerns	Minor issues, resolvable	Compliance risk identified
Stakeholder support	Board, staff, families positive	Mixed, manageable	Active opposition

Approved: ______________________________

Board Resolution Template: AI Governance Adoption

RESOLVED, that the Board of [Organization Name] hereby authorizes the formation of an AI Governance Committee with authority to evaluate, pilot, and recommend AI technologies for [facility/portfolio], subject to the following constraints:

1. AI deployments shall not exceed Level ____ without separate Board approval.
2. Initial pilot investment shall not exceed $________.
3. The Committee shall report to the Board [monthly/quarterly] on progress, expenditures, and risk assessments.
4. No AI system shall be deployed without a signed Business Associate Agreement (if PHI is involved), verified compliance with applicable federal and state regulations, and documented human oversight processes.
5. The Committee shall include representatives from clinical operations, IT, finance, legal/compliance, and frontline staff.

FURTHER RESOLVED, that the Executive Sponsor for AI implementation shall be

____

Adopted: ______________________________

Chair signature: ______________________________

SECTION 6: MATURITY MODEL SELF-ASSESSMENT

> *Assess before Sprint; reassess every 90 days. See Senior Housing: The AI Gap Chapter 12.*

Level Definitions

Level	Name	Description
0	Governance Theater	AI committee exists, no tools deployed, permanent study mode
1	Pilot Stage	1–3 AI tools on a single unit, learning mode
2	Department Scale	Multiple units using AI, one segment operational, measurable ROI
3	Enterprise Deployment	Facility-wide implementation, integrated workflows, staff competency
4	Multi-Site Optimization	Standardized across portfolio, continuous improvement, industry leadership

Diagnostic Questionnaire

Level 0 Indicators

- ☐ AI committee meets regularly but has never deployed a tool
- ☐ Multiple vendor demos completed with no vendor selected
- ☐ "We're still researching" has been the status for 6+ months
- ☐ No budget specifically allocated for AI deployment
- ☐ No executive sponsor personally committed to implementation

Count: ____________________

Level 1 Indicators

- ☐ At least one AI tool deployed operationally (not just demo)
- ☐ Pilot running on a specific unit with defined metrics
- ☐ Staff actively using AI tool (not just installed)
- ☐ Baseline metrics captured before deployment
- ☐ Regular progress reporting to committee

Count: ____________________

Level 2 Indicators

- ☐ AI deployed across multiple units or departments
- ☐ At least one use case showing measurable, documented ROI
- ☐ Staff training program established and repeatable
- ☐ Integration with core systems (EHR, billing) functioning
- ☐ Scale decision made and executed based on pilot data

Count: ______________________

Level 3 Indicators

- ☐ AI integrated into standard workflows facility-wide
- ☐ Staff competency with AI tools is part of onboarding
- ☐ Multiple AI use cases deployed simultaneously
- ☐ ROI tracking dashboard operational and reviewed monthly
- ☐ Governance framework manages AI risk as ongoing operations

Count: ______________________

Level 4 Indicators

- ☐ AI deployment standardized across multiple facilities
- ☐ New acquisitions rapidly adopt your AI tools
- ☐ Organization contributes to industry thought leadership on AI
- ☐ Vendor product development influenced by your feedback
- ☐ AI expertise is a recognized organizational competency

Count: ______________________

Success Metric Thresholds by Level

Metric	Level 1	Level 2	Level 3	Level 4
AI tools deployed	1–3	3–5	5+	5+ standardized
Units with active AI	1	2–4	Facility-wide	Portfolio-wide
Staff daily usage rate	>50% on pilot unit	>70% on deployed units	>80% facility-wide	>80% all sites
Documented ROI	Tracked, not required	Positive for 1+ use case	Positive across facility	Positive portfolio-wide
Staff satisfaction with AI	≥3.0/5	≥3.5/5	≥4.0/5	≥4.0/5
Training program	Ad hoc	Repeatable	Integrated into onboarding	Standardized portfolio
Governance maturity	Committee formed	Regular reporting	Risk management framework	Continuous improvement
Data quality score	Baseline established	>80% critical fields	>90% critical fields	>95% all fields

> *If you think you're at Level 2 but can't demonstrate all Level 2 characteristics, you're probably Level 1.*

Current Level Assessment

Assessment Date: ______________________

Current Level: ______________________

Gap Analysis

Capability Required	Current State	Gap	Action Required	Owner	Deadline
___	___	___	___	___	___
___	___	___	___	___	___
___	___	___	___	___	___
___	___	___	___	___	___

Advancement Planning Template

Moving from Level 0 → Level 1 (Typical timeline: 3–6 months)

Milestone	Action	Target Date	Status
Executive sponsor assigned	Name an individual, not a committee	____	☐
Budget approved	$25K–$75K for pilot	____	☐
Pain point selected	One use case, measurable	____	☐
Vendor selected	Using Section 2 evaluation	____	☐
90-Day Sprint launched	Section 3 execution	____	☐
Pilot live on one unit	Technology deployed, staff trained	____	☐

Moving from Level 1 → Level 2 (Typical timeline: 6–12 months)

Milestone	Action	Target Date	Status
Scale decision made	Chapter 15 framework applied	____	☐
Second unit deployed	Expansion from pilot	____	☐
ROI documented	Measured, not projected	____	☐
Training program formalized	Repeatable, role-specific	____	☐
EHR integration verified	Bidirectional data flow confirmed	____	☐
Second use case piloted	New AI application tested	____	☐

Moving from Level 2 → Level 3 (Typical timeline: 12–24 months)

Milestone	Action	Target Date	Status
Facility-wide deployment plan	Budget, timeline, unit sequence	____	☐
AI in onboarding	New staff trained on AI tools from day one	____	☐
Multiple use cases operational	3+ AI tools in daily use	____	☐
ROI dashboard live	Monthly tracking, executive review	____	☐
Governance framework operational	Risk management as BAU, not project	____	☐

Moving from Level 3 → Level 4 (Typical timeline: 12–24 months)

Milestone	Action	Target Date	Status
Portfolio standardization plan	Common tools, processes, metrics	___	☐
Acquisition integration playbook	AI deployment part of M&A process	___	☐
Industry engagement	Conference presentations, peer sharing	___	☐
Vendor partnership	Product feedback loop, early access	___	☐
Continuous improvement cycle	Quarterly optimization reviews	___	☐

Quarterly Reassessment Tracker

Date	Level	Change	Key Progress	Barriers
___	___	—	___	___
___	___	↑↓→	___	___
___	___	↑↓→	___	___
___	___	↑↓→	___	___

> *Typical advancement: 6–24 months per level. Levels cannot be skipped. Most operators: Level 0–1.*

SECTION 7: ROI CALCULATORS & FINANCIAL TOOLS

ROI Formula Reference

- ROI % = ((Benefits − Costs) / Costs) × 100
- Payback Period = Total Costs / Monthly Benefits
- Time horizon: 24 months recommended for decision-making; track monthly

Calculator 1: Cost of Non-Implementation

What does it cost your facility to NOT deploy AI? Use this to build the initial business case.

Falls

Metric	Your Facility	Industry Average
Total falls per year	___	1.5–3.0 per bed/year
Falls with injury	___	30–50% of total falls
Hospitalizations from falls	___	10–20% of injuries
Average hospital transfer cost	$___	$35,000–$50,000
Average liability claim	$___	$40,000–$100,000
Claims filed per year	___	Varies
Annual fall-related cost	$___	___

Staffing

Metric	Your Facility	Industry Average
CNA turnover rate	___%	75–100%
RN/LPN turnover rate	___%	40–60%
Cost per CNA hire	$___	$3,000–$5,000
Cost per RN hire	$___	$40,000–$80,000
Agency shifts per month	___	___
Agency premium per shift	$___	$200–$500 above regular
Overtime hours per month	___	___
Annual excess staffing cost	$___	___

Documentation Burden

Metric	Your Facility	Industry Average
Nurses on staff	____	____
Documentation time per shift	____ min	90–120 min
Loaded nurse hourly rate	$____	$35–$55
Annual documentation labor cost	$____	____
Documentation errors per month	____	____
Rework time per error	____ min	15–30 min

Competitive Position

Metric	Your Facility	Industry Average
Census/occupancy rate	____%	80–85%
Empty beds × daily rate × 365	$____	____
Admissions lost to competitors using AI	____	Estimate
Revenue per lost admission	$____	____

Total Annual Cost of Non-Implementation: $

> *If this number is $200,000+ (common for a 100-bed facility), the question isn't whether you can afford AI — it's whether you can afford not to deploy it.*

Calculator 2: Fall Detection ROI

Costs

One-Time

Item	Amount
Vendor implementation	$____
Hardware installation	$____
IT integration	$____
Staff training	$____
Total One-Time	$____

Annual Recurring

Item	Amount
Vendor subscription (____ beds × $____/bed)	$____
Maintenance/support	$____
IT ongoing support	$____
Total Annual	$____

2-Year Total Cost: $ ______________________________

Benefits

Liability Claims Reduction	Current	With AI (20–30% reduction)
Falls per year	____	____
% resulting in claims	____%	____%
Average claim cost	$____	$____
Annual fall claim cost	$____	$____

Annual benefit from claims reduction: $

____

Census protection (prevented move-outs):

____

Total Annual Benefits: $ ______________________________

2-Year ROI: ______________________________

> *Sensitivity (20% lower benefits): Adjusted ROI ____% — Still acceptable? ☐Yes ☐No*

Calculator 3: AI Documentation ROI

Costs

One-Time Item	Amount
Vendor implementation	$____
EHR integration	$____
Training (____ nurses × ____ hrs. × $____/hr.)	$____
Total One-Time	$____

Benefits

Documentation Time Savings	Current	With AI (25–35% reduction)
Nurses on staff	____	____
Doc time per shift	____ min	____ min
Shifts per year	____	____
Nurse hourly rate (loaded)	$____	$____
Annual doc cost	$____	$____

Annual time savings value: $ ______________________________

Retention Benefit	Amount
Turnover reduction	____%
Hires avoided × cost per hire ($40K–$80K RN)	$____/yr

2-Year ROI: ______________________________

Calculator 4: Staffing Optimization ROI

COSTS: One-time $ ______________________________

Category	Current	With AI	Annual Savings
Overstaffing	$____	$____ (____%)	$____
Agency shifts	$____	$____ (____%)	$____
Overtime	$____	$____ (____%)	$____
Compliance penalties avoided	$____	$____	$____

2-Year ROI: ______________________________

Calculator 5: Enterprise Deployment Financial Model

Use after successful pilot to project facility-wide ROI.

Year	Investment	Cumulative Benefits	Net Position	Cumulative ROI
Year 1 (Pilot + Dept)	$____	$____	$____	____%
Year 2 (Enterprise)	$____	$____	$____	____%
Year 3 (Optimization)	$____	$____	$____	____%

Sensitivity Analysis

Scenario	Benefits Assumption	3-Year ROI	Payback	Decision
Optimistic	120% of projected	____%	____ mo.	____
Base case	100% of projected	____%	____ mo.	____
Conservative	80% of projected	____%	____ mo.	____
Worst case	60% of projected	____%	____ mo.	____

> *If the worst-case scenario still a shows positive ROI within 24 months, the investment is defensible.*

Baseline Metrics Tracking Template

Facility: ____________________

Category	Metric	Value
Falls (12 mo.)	Total falls	____
	Falls with injury	____
	Hospitalizations from falls	____
	Avg response time	____ min
	Claims filed	____
	Claim costs paid	$____
Staff	Doc time per shift (nurses)	____ min
	Overtime hrs./month	____
	Agency shifts/month	____
Turnover	CNA turnover	____%
	LPN turnover	____%
	RN turnover	____%
Quality	CMS Star Rating	____
	Survey citations	____
	30-day readmission rate	____%

Financial	Revenue per bed	$____
	Labor % of revenue	____%
	Operating margin	____%

Monthly Pilot Tracking Dashboard

Month	Primary Metric 1	Primary Metric 2	Staff Usage	Staff Satisfaction	Spend vs. Budget	Issues Open
Baseline	____	____	N/A	N/A	$0	N/A
Month 1	____	____	____%	____/5	$____	____
Month 2	____	____	____%	____/5	$____	____
Month 3	____	____	____%	____/5	$____	____

SECTION 8: DATA QUALITY & INTEGRATION TOOLS

> *See Senior Housing: The AI Gap Chapters 7 (Interoperability) and 8 (Data Quality).*

8.1 Integration Evaluation Checklist

Complete before signing any vendor contract. The Five Questions That Matter (from Chapter 7) plus the comprehensive 20+ question evaluation.

The Five Questions That Matter

These five questions separate successful facilities from those that fail. Get written answers before proceeding.

1. Reference Verification

"Can I speak with a customer who runs my exact EHR version and successfully integrated your tool?"

- ☐ Vendor provided reference with my EHR platform: ___________________
- ☐ Reference confirmed: EHR version matches ours
- ☐ Reference confirmed: Integration works as described
- ☐ Reference contact name/facility: ___________________

> *Not "we integrate with PointClickCare." Your specific platform, version number, and a contactable reference. If the vendor can't provide this, you're a beta tester.*

2. Data Flow Specifics

"What data flows automatically, and what requires manual entry?"

- ☐ Vendor provided field-by-field data flow list
- ☐ Critical clinical data flows automatically: ☐ Yes ☐ No
- ☐ Manual entry requirements identified: ___________________
- ☐ Staff impact of manual entry assessed: acceptable ☐ Yes ☐ No

> *If critical clinical data requires manual entry, integration is incomplete, and your staff will revolt.*

3. Bidirectional Flow

"Is data flow bidirectional? Can the AI tool pull data from our EHR AND write updates back?"

- ☐ AI reads from EHR: ☐ Yes ☐ No
- ☐ AI writes back to EHR: ☐ Yes ☐ No
- ☐ Both directions confirmed in writing

> *One-way data flow creates the duplicate-entry problem that kills adoption.*

4. Timeline and Exit

"Provide the integration timeline and cost, in writing, with an exit clause if it fails."

- ☐ Written integration timeline: ____ days
- ☐ Integration cost: $____
- ☐ Exit clause if integration fails: ☐ Yes ☐ No
- ☐ Contractual commitment: "Integration complete within ____ days or contract voidable"

> *"Typically, 30-60 days" is not acceptable. You need a contractual commitment.*

5. Responsibility

"Who handles integration work?"

- ☐ Vendor handles with your IT support (BEST)
- ☐ Shared responsibility (ACCEPTABLE — clarify division in writing)
- ☐ Your IT team builds custom integration (RED FLAG for most facilities)

> *If you have part-time IT support and the vendor expects you to build custom integration, that's a dealbreaker.*

Comprehensive Integration Evaluation (20+ Questions)

Compatibility (5 questions)

- ☐ What EHR platforms has the vendor successfully integrated with? List all.
- ☐ What version of our EHR is supported? Is our specific version confirmed?
- ☐ What integration standards are used (HL7, FHIR, proprietary API)?
- ☐ Does the integration support our current network infrastructure (bandwidth, latency)?
- ☐ Are there known conflicts with other software we run (billing, scheduling, pharmacy)?

Implementation (5 questions)

- ☐ What is the step-by-step implementation timeline with milestones?
- ☐ What are the technical prerequisites we must complete before integration begins?
- ☐ What testing protocol is used before go-live? Who signs off?
- ☐ What is the rollback plan if integration fails during deployment?
- ☐ Is there a parallel-run period where old and new systems operate simultaneously?

Technical (5 questions)

- ☐ How is data synchronized — real-time, batch (how often), or on-demand?
- ☐ What happens to data flow if the AI system goes down? Does the EHR continue normally?
- ☐ How are software updates to either system handled without breaking integration?
- ☐ What monitoring is in place to detect integration failures?

- ☐ What is the vendor's average integration downtime per month?

Security (3 questions)

- ☐ How is data encrypted during transfer between systems?
- ☐ What authentication is used for system-to-system communication?
- ☐ How is the integration point included in penetration testing and security audits?

Support (4 questions)

- ☐ Who is the dedicated integration support contact?
- ☐ What is the response time for integration-related issues?
- ☐ How are integration problems diagnosed — vendor-side, EHR-side, or joint?
- ☐ What is the vendor's integration success rate across all customers?

Overall Integration Assessment:

☐ Green: All Five Questions answered satisfactorily, comprehensive checklist clear

☐ Yellow: Minor gaps identified, resolvable before contract signing

☐ Red: Critical gaps — do not proceed until resolved

8.2 Data Quality Assessment

Complete during Week 1 of the 90-Day Sprint. Estimated time: 4–8 hours.

Step 1: Identify Critical Data Fields for Your Use Case

Your Pilot Use Case	Critical Data Fields
Fall detection	Mobility status, fall history, medications affecting balance, room assignment, weight
Clinical documentation	Cognitive status, diagnoses, medications, care plan, baseline assessments
Staffing optimization	Census, acuity levels, staff schedules, shift patterns, overtime history
Resident engagement	Cognitive status, interests, communication preferences, family contacts
Billing/revenue cycle	Diagnosis codes, service documentation, payer information, care levels

List YOUR critical fields: ______________________________

Step 2: Sample Audit (30–50 Records)

Pull a random sample of 30–50 resident records. For each critical field, assess:

Critical Field	Records Complete (n/50)	Completeness %	Format Consistent?	Accuracy Verified?
____________	___/50	___%	☐Y☐N	☐Y☐N
____________	___/50	___%	☐Y☐N	☐Y☐N
____________	___/50	___%	☐Y☐N	☐Y☐N
____________	___/50	___%	☐Y☐N	☐Y☐N
____________	___/50	___%	☐Y☐N	☐Y☐N
____________	___/50	___%	☐Y☐N	☐Y☐N

Step 3: Score Against Thresholds

Metric	Your Score	Deploy Now (>80%)	Limited Deploy (60–80%)	Fix First (<60%)
Completeness (critical fields)	___%	☐	☐	☐
Format consistency	___%	☐	☐	☐
Accuracy (sample verified)	___%	☐	☐	☐
Duplicate record rate	___%	<5% OK	5–15% concern	>15% fix first

Step 4: Determine Your Path

If >80% completeness in critical fields: Proceed with AI deployment. Monitor data quality during pilot. Establish prospective standards for new data entry.

If 60–80% completeness: Limited deployment on well-documented units or residents. Identify which units/residents have complete data and pilot there. Establish data entry standards immediately.

If <60% completeness: Data cleanup required before AI deployment. Focus only on critical fields for your specific use case. Standardize prospectively (new data going forward), not retroactively. Estimated cost: $5,000–$15,000 (minimum viable approach) vs. $30,000–$130,000 (comprehensive cleanup).

Step 5: Minimum Viable Data Quality Action Plan

Action	Owner	Deadline	Status
Define required data fields for pilot use case	____	____	☐
Configure EHR validation rules for required fields	____	____	☐

Train staff on data entry standards (prospective)	____	____	☐
Clean critical fields for pilot unit residents only	____	____	☐
Establish ongoing data quality monitoring	____	____	☐
Assign data quality responsibility to specific role	____	____	☐

> *Don't clean all historical data. Establish standards for new data entry going forward, configure system validation to enforce them, and let historical messy data age out of relevance.*

8.3 Common Data Quality Problems: Diagnostic Guide

Use this to identify which data quality issues exist in your facility.

Problem	How to Spot It	Impact on AI	Fix Complexity
Missing data	Blank fields in critical records; AI works for some residents but not others	AI ignores residents without data; staff perceive AI as arbitrary	Low–Medium: Prospective entry standards
Inconsistent formats	Same item documented multiple ways (Tylenol/acetaminophen/APAP)	AI can't identify patterns across records	Medium: Standardize terminology, build crosswalk
Duplicate records	Same resident has multiple records (common after hospital readmission)	AI misreads length of stay, can't track trends	Medium–High: Deduplication process
Outdated information	Resolved conditions still listed as active	AI generates false positives, staff lose trust	Low: Regular record review schedule
Inaccurate data	Transposed digits, wrong codes, copy-paste errors	Compounds across population; degrades AI calibration	Medium: Spot audits, validation rules

SECTION 9: THE STATE REGULATORY LANDSCAPE

> *State-level complement to the federal regulatory framework in Senior Housing: The AI Gap Chapter 16.*

The Four Tiers of State AI Regulation

Tier	Characteristics	States
1: Comprehensive	Broad AI governance, disclosure mandates, impact assessments	Colorado, California
2: Healthcare-Specific	AI disclosure for providers, clinical decision limits	Texas, Illinois, New Mexico, Florida (proposed)
3: Consumer Privacy	Profiling opt-out, data protection impact assessments	IN, KY, RI, VA, CT, UT, MT, OR
4: Proposed/Study	Bills introduced, study commissions, task forces	Pennsylvania, others

Key State Requirements

Tier 1: Colorado AI Act (In Effect)

Covers "high-risk AI systems" in healthcare, housing, insurance decisions.

Requirements: Disclosure when AI makes consequential decisions; annual impact assessments; anti-bias controls; 3-year record-keeping.

Penalties: AG enforcement, deceptive trade practice.

Senior housing must:

- ☐ Identify high-risk AI systems
- ☐ Obtain impact assessments from vendors
- ☐ Implement disclosure protocols
- ☐ Verify bias testing
- ☐ Maintain 3-year documentation

Tier 1: California (Multiple Laws, January 1, 2026)

AB 489: AI cannot imply it's a licensed healthcare provider. AB 3030 / SB 1120: Disclose AI use in clinical decisions. SB 942: AI transparency for large providers (1M+ monthly users).

Senior housing must:

- ☐ Clear AI disclosure in resident-facing health communication
- ☐ No AI misrepresentation as licensed staff

- ☐ Crisis safeguards for companion AI

Tier 2: Texas TRAIGA (January 1, 2026)

Senior housing must:

- ☐ Written disclosure if AI assists clinical decisions
- ☐ Document human review of AI recommendations
- ☐ Train staff on disclosure requirements

Tier 2: Illinois (August 1, 2025)

Senior housing must:

- ☐ No AI conducting therapy independently
- ☐ Therapist maintains control
- ☐ AI for admin/engagement OK; therapeutic use requires professional involvement

Tier 2: New Mexico (November 18, 2025)

Senior housing must:

- ☐ Consent obtained for AI in mental health contexts
- ☐ AI risks disclosed

Tier 3: Consumer Privacy States

Indiana, Kentucky, Rhode Island (January 1, 2026), Virginia, Connecticut, Utah, others.

Senior housing must:

- ☐ Determine if AI = "profiling" under state law
- ☐ Confirm HIPAA exemption covers your use
- ☐ Conduct DPIAs for high-risk AI
- ☐ Provide opt-out if required

Compliance Quick Reference Matrix

State	Law	Effective	Key Requirement	Penalty
Colorado	AI Act	In effect	Disclosure, impact assessments, anti-bias	AG enforcement
California	AB 489, AB 3030, SB 1120	Jan 1, 2026	Healthcare disclosure, chatbot safeguards	Varies
Texas	TRAIGA, SB 1188	Jan/Sept 2025–26	Written disclosure, practitioner review	Licensing + AG

Illinois	MH AI restrictions	Aug 1, 2025	No independent AI therapy	Licensing
New Mexico	Reg 16.27.18.24	Nov 18, 2025	Informed consent for AI in MH	Board enforcement
Florida	SB 794	Proposed 2026	24hr advance consent for AI recording	TBD
IN, KY, RI	Consumer privacy	Jan 1, 2026	Profiling opt-out, DPIAs	AG enforcement
Utah	AI Policy Act	In effect	Disclosure, learning laboratory	Regulatory sandbox

Multi-State Compliance Strategy

Strategy	Description	Best For
Strictest Standard	Comply with most stringent state (CO/CA) everywhere	Operators in CO/CA wanting unified approach
State-by-State	Customize per state	Operators with in-house legal
Hybrid (recommended)	Core baseline everywhere + enhanced in strict states	Most multi-state operators

Multi-State Compliance Worksheet

Your facilities are in these states: ____________

State	Tier	Key Requirements	Current Compliance	Gap	Action Needed
___	___	___	☐ Full ☐ Partial ☐ None	___	___
___	___	___	☐ Full ☐ Partial ☐ None	___	___
___	___	___	☐ Full ☐ Partial ☐ None	___	___
___	___	___	☐ Full ☐ Partial ☐ None	___	___

Regulatory Monitoring Framework

Quarterly:

- ☐ Review proposed legislation in operating states
- ☐ Update compliance matrix
- ☐ Assess current AI deployments against new requirements

Semi-Annually:

- ☐ Full compliance audit by state
- ☐ Review vendor compliance certifications
- ☐ Update staff training on disclosure requirements

Annually:

- ☐ Legal counsel comprehensive review
- ☐ Board briefing on regulatory landscape changes
- ☐ Strategic planning for anticipated regulation
- ☐ Update all disclosure documents and consent forms

SECTION 10: STAKEHOLDER COMMUNICATION TEMPLATES

> *See Senior Housing: The AI Gap Chapter 13: The Stakeholder Trust Framework.*

Communication Timeline

Use this grid to plan when each stakeholder group receives communication at each implementation phase.

Phase	Staff	Families	Residents	Board	Timeline
Pre-Sprint	Informal awareness	Nothing yet	Nothing yet	Budget approval request	2–4 weeks before Sprint
Sprint Start (Week 1)	Kickoff announcement	Nothing yet	Nothing yet	Sprint launch notification	Day 1
Vendor Selected (Week 3)	"We're evaluating tools"	Nothing yet	Nothing yet	Vendor selection report	Week 3
Pre-Pilot (Week 4)	Training schedule + FAQ	Family FAQ document	Resident info sheet	Pilot design summary	Week 4
Pilot Launch (Week 5)	Go-live communication	Family letter or email	Posted information	Pilot launch confirmation	Day 31
Mid-Pilot (Week 8)	Progress update + feedback request	Update if appropriate	Nothing unless change	Mid-pilot assessment	Day 60
Post-Pilot (Week 12)	Results + decision	Results summary	Update on next steps	Scale decision presentation	Day 90
Scale Decision	Expansion plan + timeline	Expansion notification	Updated information	Board briefing + vote	Week 13+

10.1 Staff Announcement: AI Implementation Kickoff

TO: All [facility/unit] staff

FROM: [Executive Sponsor name and title]

RE: AI Technology Pilot — [Tool Name]

DATE: ____________________

We are launching a pilot of [tool name] on [unit] starting [date]. This technology [brief description — e.g., "helps detect falls faster" or "reduces documentation time"].

What this means for you:

- [Specific impact on their workflow — positive framing]
- Training will be provided [dates/format]
- This is a 90-day pilot — your feedback will determine whether we expand

What this does NOT mean:

- This is not replacing anyone's job
- This is not monitoring your performance
- This is a tool to help you do your job better

Your role: [Specific expectations — use the tool, provide honest feedback, report issues]

Questions? Contact [name] at [contact info] or attend the Q&A session on [date/time].

> *Your input matters. This pilot succeeds or fails based on your feedback.*

10.2 Staff Fear-Response Guide

Use these responses in staff meetings, one-on-ones, and Q&A sessions. See Chapter 13 for the strategic framework.

Fear 1: "AI Will Replace My Job"

Response: "AI won't replace you. The staffing shortage means we're desperate for workers, not looking to eliminate positions. AI helps you work more efficiently so you can spend more time on patient care, which is why you became a nurse. We're not eliminating jobs; we're making jobs less stressful."

Support with data:

- Show turnover rates: "We're hiring, not firing"
- Workforce projections: 1.3 million additional workers needed by 2030
- Reference facilities using AI that are hiring, not laying off

Fear 2: "Technology Will Monitor Everything I Do"

Response: "We're monitoring resident safety, not employee performance. Fall detection tracks residents, not staff. Documentation AI helps you chart faster; it doesn't judge your work."

Be specific about what IS monitored:

- GPS in home care apps verifies visits but doesn't track off-hours
- Documentation timestamps ensure charting is done but don't measure speed
- Explain why monitoring exists (compliance, safety) and its limits

Fear 3: "This Will Make My Job Harder, Not Easier"

Response: "You're right to be skeptical. We've piloted this first to make sure it actually helps before rolling it out. If it makes your job harder, we won't deploy it facility-wide. We need your honest feedback during the pilot so we can fix problems before scaling."

Support with evidence:

- Documentation time savings (30% less charting time)
- Testimonials from other facilities
- Commitment to abandon if it doesn't help

Fear 4: "I'm Not Tech-Savvy Enough"

Response: "We'll train you thoroughly, and we'll have support available. If you can use a smartphone, you can use this system. We're choosing tools designed for busy caregivers, not IT professionals."

Support structure:

- Extra training time available
- Buddy systems pairing tech-averse staff with comfortable peers
- Patient troubleshooting support — no question is too basic

10.3 Family FAQ Document

[Facility Name] — AI Technology Information for Families

Q: What AI technology are you using?

A: We are piloting [tool name], which [brief, plain-language description]. It is designed to [benefit].

Q: Why are you using AI?

A: To improve [specific benefit] for your loved one. [Specific data point — e.g., "Studies show AI fall detection reduces response times from several minutes to under 90 seconds."]

Q: Is my family member's information safe?

A: Yes. The system is HIPAA-compliant. [Vendor name] has signed a Business Associate Agreement ensuring your loved one's data is protected. Data is encrypted and accessible only to authorized staff.

Q: Will AI replace human caregivers?

A: No. AI assists our staff — it does not replace them. [Example: "Nurses still respond to every fall; the AI helps them respond faster."]

Q: What data is collected?

A: [Specific to your AI tool — e.g., "The fall detection system uses sensors to detect fall events only. It does not record conversations or monitor daily activities."]

Q: Who has access to the data?

A: Only authorized clinical and administrative staff at our facility. The vendor accesses data only for technical support, under a strict HIPAA Business Associate Agreement.

Q: How long is data kept?

A: [Your data retention policy — e.g., "Data is retained for the duration of your family member's stay plus [X] years, consistent with state and federal record retention requirements."]

Q: Can my family member opt out?

A: [Yes/No, with details. If yes: "Contact [name] at [phone/email] to discuss opt-out options and any impact on care services."]

Q: How can I learn more or share concerns?

A: Contact [name] at [phone/email]. We welcome your questions at any time.

10.4 Resident Information Sheet

[Facility Name] — New Technology: [Tool Name]

(Use plain language, large font for posting)

What is it? [1–2 sentences, plain language]

What does it do? [Specific benefit in resident terms]

What does it NOT do? [Address top concern — e.g., "It does not listen to your conversations or watch you throughout the day."]

Do I have to participate? [Yes/No and why]

Who can I talk to? ____________________

10.5 Resident AI Disclosure Template — Admission Documents

For inclusion in admission packets when AI systems are in use.

AI Technology Disclosure

[Facility Name] uses the following AI-assisted technologies as part of our commitment to resident safety and quality care:

Technology	Purpose	What It Does	What It Does NOT Do
[Tool name]	[e.g., Fall safety]	[e.g., Detects falls and alerts staff]	[e.g., Record conversations or monitor daily activities]
[Tool name]	[e.g., Documentation]	[e.g., Helps nurses document care faster]	[e.g., Make clinical decisions without nurse review]

All AI systems are overseen by qualified clinical staff. No AI system replaces human judgment in clinical decisions. Your data is protected under HIPAA and our privacy policies.

Questions? Contact our AI Implementation Coordinator:

____

Resident/Representative Acknowledgment:

10.6 Resident Opt-In/Opt-Out Form

[Facility Name] — AI Technology Participation

Resident Name:

I have been informed about the following AI technologies in use at [Facility Name]:

Technology	I consent to participate	I decline participation
[Tool 1]	☐	☐
[Tool 2]	☐	☐
[Tool 3]	☐	☐

If declining: I understand that opting out of [specific technology] may affect [specific impact — e.g., "the speed of fall detection response in my room"]. Staff will continue to provide all required care services regardless of my AI technology preferences.

I understand that:

- I may change my decision at any time by contacting

- My care will not be reduced because of my decision
- My data is protected under HIPAA regardless of participation

Signature:

Representative (if applicable):

10.7 Training Curriculum Template

Role-Specific Training Plan

Role	Training Focus	Duration	Format	When
Nursing (RN/LPN)	Clinical oversight, AI validation, override procedures	2–3 hours	Hands-on + classroom	3–5 days before pilot launch
CNAs/Aides	Daily use, basic troubleshooting, reporting issues	1–2 hours	Hands-on demonstration	1–3 days before pilot launch
Administrative	Reporting, data access, family communication	1 hour	Classroom/online	1 week before pilot launch
IT	Integration monitoring, troubleshooting, vendor liaison	2–4 hours	Technical training with vendor	2 weeks before pilot launch
Management	Oversight, metrics review, staff support	1 hour	Briefing	1 week before pilot launch

Training Session Outline (Clinical Staff)

Hour 1: Understanding the Technology

- What the AI does and doesn't do (15 min)
- How it fits your workflow (15 min)
- Demonstration by vendor (30 min)

Hour 2: Hands-On Practice

- Guided practice with real scenarios (30 min)
- Practice overriding/validating AI recommendations (15 min)
- Troubleshooting common issues (15 min)

Hour 3 (Nurses Only): Clinical Oversight

- When to trust vs. question AI output (15 min)
- Override documentation requirements (15 min)
- Escalation procedures (15 min)
- Q&A (15 min)

Competency Assessment Checklist

Staff Name: ______________________________

Competency	Demonstrated	Needs Practice	Not Assessed
Can log in and access AI tool	☐	☐	☐
Can perform primary task with AI tool	☐	☐	☐
Can identify when AI output needs review	☐	☐	☐
Can override AI recommendation when appropriate	☐	☐	☐
Can report technical issues through proper channel	☐	☐	☐
Can explain AI to residents/families in plain language	☐	☐	☐
Understands what data AI collects	☐	☐	☐
Knows escalation procedures	☐	☐	☐

Assessment result: ☐ Competent ☐ Requires additional training (schedule:
____

Assessor: ______________________________

10.8 Board Briefing Template

AI Implementation Update — [Date]

Status: [On Track / At Risk / Off Track / Complete]

Key Metrics

Metric	Baseline	Current	Target	Trend
___	___	___	___	↑↓→
___	___	___	___	↑↓→
___	___	___	___	↑↓→

Financial Summary

Item	Amount
Investment to date	$___
Benefits realized	$___
Projected annual ROI	___%
Budget remaining	$___
Variance from approved budget	___%

Stakeholder Pulse

Group	Sentiment	Key Feedback
Staff	☐ Positive ☐ Mixed ☐ Negative	___
Residents	☐ Positive ☐ Mixed ☐ Negative	___
Families	☐ Positive ☐ Mixed ☐ Negative	___

Risks & Mitigation

Risk	Likelihood	Impact	Mitigation	Status
___	H/M/L	H/M/L	___	___
___	H/M/L	H/M/L	___	___

Compliance Status

- Federal (HIPAA/FDA/CMS): ☐ Compliant ☐ Issues identified
- State: ☐ Compliant ☐ Issues identified
- BAA status: ☐ Current ☐ Needs renewal

Decision Required

Recommendation

10.9 Monthly Stakeholder Update Template

AI Implementation Monthly Update — [Month/Year]

Progress: ____________________

Results this month: ____________________

Challenges: ____________________

Coming next month: ____________________

How to provide feedback: ____________________

SECTION 11: COMPLIANCE & INCIDENT RESPONSE

> *See Senior Housing: The AI Gap Chapter 16 for the strategic framework. Three non-negotiable principles: No BAA = No Contract | No FDA Verification = No Clinical AI | No Human Oversight = No CMS Compliance.*

11.1 HIPAA Vendor Compliance Verification Questionnaire

Complete before signing any contract with a vendor that handles PHI. Eight categories of written questions — vendor must provide written responses.

Category 1: Business Associate Agreement

- ☐ Does the vendor provide a BAA? (If no, STOP — do not proceed if PHI is involved)
- ☐ Does the BAA specify permitted uses of PHI (services only)?
- ☐ Does the BAA prohibit use of PHI for marketing, research, or sale?
- ☐ Does the BAA include breach notification requirements (24–72 hour timeframe)?
- ☐ Does the BAA specify data return and destruction procedures on termination?

Category 2: Encryption and Data Security

- ☐ Is data at rest encrypted with AES-256?
- ☐ Is data in transit encrypted with TLS 1.2+?
- ☐ Are API communications authenticated and secured?
- ☐ Does the vendor maintain audit logs of all PHI access?
- ☐ Is breach detection technology in place?

Category 3: Access Controls

- ☐ Does the vendor enforce role-based access controls?
- ☐ Is multi-factor authentication required for all PHI access?
- ☐ Are automatic session timeouts configured?
- ☐ How many vendor employees can access your facility's PHI? Number: ____
- ☐ What is the vendor's process for employee background checks?

Category 4: Sub-Processor Disclosure

- ☐ Does the vendor use cloud providers (AWS, Azure, Google Cloud)?
- ☐ List all sub-processors handling PHI:

____

☐ Does the vendor have BAAs with each sub-processor?

☐ Can you verify the BAA chain extends to all parties handling PHI?

☐ Where are data centers located? ☐ U.S. only ☐ International (RED FLAG)

Category 5: AI Training Data

☐ Is your facility's PHI used to train AI models? ☐ Yes ☐ No

☐ If yes, through what legal mechanism? ☐ De-identification ☐ Authorization ☐ Limited data set ☐ Other

☐ Can you opt out of having your data used for model training?

☐ Are AI training datasets subject to the same HIPAA protections as operational data?

Category 6: Compliance Certifications

☐ Does the vendor hold SOC 2 Type II certification? Date of last report: ____

☐ Does the vendor hold HITRUST certification? ☐ Yes ☐ No

☐ Does the vendor conduct annual penetration testing? Date of last test: ____

☐ Does the vendor carry cyber liability insurance? Amount: $____

☐ Will the vendor provide copies of certifications and audit reports?

Category 7: Incident Response

☐ Does the vendor have a documented breach response plan?

☐ What is the vendor's breach notification timeframe? ____ hours

☐ What information will the vendor provide in a breach notification?

☐ Will the vendor assist with HHS and individual notification?

☐ Has the vendor experienced a data breach in the past 3 years? ☐ Yes ☐ No (verify at HHS breach portal)

Category 8: FDA and Clinical AI

☐ Does the AI tool make or influence clinical decisions? ☐ Yes ☐ No

☐ If yes, does the tool have FDA clearance? Clearance number: ____

☐ Have you verified clearance in the FDA database (not just vendor marketing)?

☐ If vendor claims FDA clearance is not required, what is their reasoning?

____

☐ Does the vendor maintain documentation of clinical validation studies?

Overall Vendor Compliance Assessment:

☐ Pass: All categories satisfactory. Proceed with contract negotiation.

☐ Conditional: Minor gaps in 1–2 categories. Vendor must resolve before signing.

☐ Fail: Critical gaps (missing BAA, no encryption, no certifications). Do not proceed.

Assessed by: ______________________________

Legal counsel reviewed: ☐ Yes ☐ No Date:

____

11.2 FDA Clearance Verification Checklist

For any AI vendor claiming clinical capabilities.

- ☐ Vendor claims FDA clearance: ☐ Yes ☐ No ☐ Claims not needed

If vendor claims clearance:

- ☐ Obtained FDA 510(k) clearance number from vendor: ___________________
- ☐ Verified in FDA database (accessdata.fda.gov): ☐ Confirmed ☐ Not found
- ☐ Clearance matches the specific product version being offered: ☐ Yes ☐ No
- ☐ Indications for use match your intended application: ☐ Yes ☐ No

If vendor claims clearance not needed:

- ☐ Vendor provided written explanation of why
- ☐ Legal counsel reviewed and agrees: ☐ Yes ☐ No
- ☐ Tool classified as: ☐ Clinical Decision Support (CDS exempt) ☐ Administrative only ☐ Wellness/general

> *Marketing materials are not evidence. Verify every FDA claim directly in the FDA database.*

11.3 Implementation Compliance Checklist

Complete before pilot go-live.

Pre-Deployment

- ☐ BAA signed and filed
- ☐ FDA status verified (if clinical)
- ☐ State-specific requirements identified (Section 9)
- ☐ AI disclosure documents prepared for residents/families (Section 10.5)
- ☐ Staff trained on HIPAA implications of AI use
- ☐ Public AI policy in place (prohibiting PHI in ChatGPT, Gemini, etc.)
- ☐ Data governance policy adopted (Section 5.4)
- ☐ Audit trail capabilities confirmed
- ☐ Human override processes documented

During Pilot

- ☐ Monitoring for unauthorized PHI access
- ☐ Verifying AI audit trail captures all decisions
- ☐ Confirming human oversight of clinical AI recommendations
- ☐ Tracking compliance with state disclosure requirements
- ☐ Documenting any incidents or near-misses

Ongoing (Post-Deployment)

- ☐ Monthly: Review AI audit logs for anomalies
- ☐ Quarterly: Vendor compliance review (Section 4.5)
- ☐ Semi-annually: State regulatory review (Section 9)
- ☐ Annually: Comprehensive compliance audit
- ☐ Annually: BAA review and renewal
- ☐ Annually: Staff HIPAA/AI training refresh

11.4 Incident Response Protocols

PHI Breach Response

If a breach involving AI-processed PHI is discovered or suspected:

Hour 0–4: Contain

- ☐ Identify scope: What data? How many residents? How long?
- ☐ Stop the breach: Disable compromised access, isolate affected systems if needed
- ☐ Preserve evidence: Do not delete logs
- ☐ Notify: Executive sponsor, IT, legal counsel
- ☐ Contact vendor: Activate vendor incident response per BAA

Hours 4–24: Assess

- ☐ Determine if PHI was actually accessed/disclosed (vs. potential exposure)
- ☐ Identify affected individuals
- ☐ Document timeline of events
- ☐ Assess risk of harm to affected individuals
- ☐ Begin root cause analysis

Days 1–7: Investigate and Remediate

- ☐ Complete root cause analysis

☐ Implement corrective measures

☐ Prepare breach notification content

☐ Legal counsel reviews notification obligations

☐ Prepare HHS report (if 500+ individuals, report within 60 days; if <500, report by end of calendar year)

Days 7–60: Notify

☐ Notify affected individuals (within 60 days of discovery)

☐ Notify HHS (breach.hhs.gov)

☐ Notify media if 500+ individuals in a single state/jurisdiction

☐ Notify state attorney general if required by state law

☐ Document all notifications sent

AI System Failure Response

If an AI system fails, produces dangerous recommendations, or experiences significant downtime:

Immediate (0–1 hour):

☐ Activate manual backup procedures

☐ Notify affected staff: "AI system [name] is currently unavailable. Use manual procedures."

☐ Contact vendor technical support

☐ Notify executive sponsor

Short-term (1–24 hours):

☐ Assess patient safety impact

☐ Document the failure and any clinical consequences

☐ Verify manual backup procedures are working

☐ Get vendor timeline for resolution

Resolution:

☐ Vendor provides root cause analysis

☐ System testing before restoration

☐ Staff notification of system restoration

☐ Incident report filed for governance committee review

☐ Assess whether incident triggers regulatory reporting

CMS Survey Preparedness

If a CMS surveyor asks about AI technology:

Be prepared to demonstrate:

- ☐ AI does not replace required clinical assessments
- ☐ Human oversight of all clinical AI recommendations is documented
- ☐ Staff can explain their clinical reasoning independent of AI
- ☐ AI system failures do not compromise required care delivery
- ☐ Resident rights are maintained (privacy, consent, opt-out if applicable)
- ☐ Documentation meets CMS requirements regardless of AI involvement

Have ready:

- ☐ BAA documentation
- ☐ AI audit trail examples
- ☐ Human override documentation
- ☐ Staff training records
- ☐ AI system policies and procedures
- ☐ Incident response plan
- ☐ Vendor compliance certifications

11.5 Trust Recovery Protocol

When AI-related incidents damage stakeholder trust. See Chapter 13: When Trust Breaks.

Step	Action	Timeline	Responsible
1. Acknowledge	State the problem without minimizing	Immediately	Executive sponsor
2. Respond	Stop deployment if safety issue; contain the problem	Immediately	Operations lead
3. Investigate	Root cause analysis	24–72 hours	Project manager + vendor
4. Correct	Implement fix or decide to stop deployment	1–2 weeks	Governance committee
5. Communicate	Explain what happened, what changed, what's next	After correction	Executive sponsor
6. Verify	Confirm fix works; monitor for recurrence	Ongoing	Operations lead

Trust Recovery Communication by Stakeholder

Staff: Be direct. Explain what happened, why, and what changes. Acknowledge their concerns were valid. Ask for continued feedback.

Families: Contact proactively (don't wait for them to call). Explain in plain language. Describe protective measures taken. Offer to discuss individually.

Residents: Simple, reassuring language. Focus on what was done to protect them. Provide contact for questions.

Board: Full incident report. Root cause analysis. Corrective actions with timeline. Risk reassessment. Recommendation (continue with modifications, pause, or stop).

> *Sometimes the best response is to stop deployment entirely. The willingness to stop builds more trust than any communication plan.*

SECTION 12: QUICK REFERENCE CARDS

12.1 LITT Framework Summary

Phase	Name	Core Question	Key Activities	Book Chapters
1	Disruption	What does AI change?	Map AI impact by care setting; assess infrastructure barriers	6, 7, 8
2	Emotion	How do people respond?	Apply 10-80-10 rule; manage culture gap; build trust	9, 10
3	Direction	What must the board decide?	Five board decisions; maturity assessment; trust framework	11, 12, 13
4	Focus	How do we execute?	90-Day AI Governance Sprint; scale decision; regulatory compliance	14, 15, 16

> *Organizations that skip phases encounter predictable failures. Phase progression is sequential.*

12.2 Five Board Decisions at a Glance

#	Decision	Core Question	Default If Not Decided
1	AI Boundaries	What can AI do?	Undefined scope → scope creep or paralysis
2	Risk Tolerance	What error rates are acceptable?	No thresholds → can't evaluate performance
3	Human Accountability	Who's responsible when AI fails?	Diffused responsibility → no one owns problems
4	Data Governance	What are the rules for data?	Ad hoc decisions → compliance risk
5	Investment Commitment	How much, for how long?	Underfunded pilots → guaranteed failure

> *All five must be decided before Phase 4 pilots begin.*

12.3 10-80-10 Rule Quick Reference

Group	Size	Characteristics	Strategy
Champions	10%	Embrace AI immediately	Leverage for proof of concept, peer influence
Moveable Middle	80%	Wait for proof, support, reassurance	Focus here — provide evidence, training, celebrate wins
Resisters	10%	Resist regardless of evidence	Don't invest heavily — set expectations, don't let them block

> *Applies to: staff, residents, families, and executives. Each group needs tailored strategies.*

12.4 90-Day AI Governance Sprint Timeline

Week	Stage	Key Activity	Deliverable
1	Stage 1	Brutal truth assessment	Current State Assessment
2		Pain point selection	Pilot Use Case Definition
3		Vendor evaluation & demos	Vendor Comparison Matrix
4		Pilot design & contract	Pilot Design Document signed
5	Stage 2	Pilot launch	System LIVE
6–7		Execution & support	Weekly Status Reports
8		Mid-pilot assessment	Continue/Adjust/Abort decision
9–10	Stage 3	Data collection & analysis	Pilot Results Report
11		Stakeholder review	Evaluation Presentation
12		SCALE DECISION	Scale / Pivot / Stop

> *Day 90 decision is mandatory. Extensions are governance theater.*

12.5 Scale Decision Quick Reference

Metric	Scale (20%+)	Pivot (10–20%)	Stop (<10%)
Primary metric improvement	✓ Strong	~ Mixed	✗ Weak
Staff adoption	>70%	40–70%	<40%
Staff satisfaction	≥3.5/5	2.5–3.4	<2.5
Technology uptime	>95%	90–95%	<90%
ROI trajectory	Positive <12 mo	Breakeven 12–24 mo	No path

12.6 Maturity Model at a Glance

Level	Name	You're Here If...	Next Step
0	Governance Theater	Committee meets, nothing deployed	Start 90-Day AI Governance Sprint
1	Pilot Stage	1–3 tools on one unit	Scale successful pilot
2	Department Scale	Multiple units, measurable ROI	Deploy facility-wide
3	Enterprise Deployment	Facility-wide, integrated workflows	Standardize across portfolio
4	Multi-Site Optimization	Portfolio-wide, industry leadership	Continuous optimization

> *Each transition: 6–24 months. Levels cannot be skipped. Most operators: Level 0–1.*

12.7 Three Non-Negotiable Compliance Principles

Principle	Rule	Consequence of Violation
No BAA = No Contract	If AI vendor handling PHI won't sign a BAA, walk away	HIPAA violation, $100–$50,000 per violation
No FDA Verification = No Clinical AI	Verify FDA clearance in FDA database, not vendor marketing	FDA enforcement: warnings, recalls, injunctions
No Human Oversight = No CMS Compliance	Document human oversight for every clinical AI system	CMS termination from Medicare/Medicaid

---

This workbook is designed for reproduction and committee use. Copy templates as needed. Update vendor and regulatory sections annually.

For the strategic frameworks behind these tools, see Senior Housing: The AI Gap — particularly Chapters 2 (LITT Framework), 3 (Failure Modes), and 14 (The 90-Day AI Governance Sprint).

This workbook is designed for reproduction and committee use.

Copy templates as needed. Update vendor and regulatory sections annually.

For the strategic frameworks behind these tools, see

Senior Housing: The AI Gap

Made in United States
Orlando, FL
04 November 2026

90201003R00044